THE EXTRAORDINARY IDEAS OF
LEONARDO DA VINCI

ALEX WOOLF
&
PAULA ZAMUDIO

ARCTURUS

Arcturus

This edition published in 2024 by Arcturus Publishing Limited
26/27 Bickels Yard, 151–153 Bermondsey Street,
London SE1 3HA

Writer: Alex Woolf
Illustrator: Paula Zamudio
Designer: Rosie Bellwood
Editors: Coffee Cup Creative, Lydia Halliday
Managing Editor: Joe Harris
Managing Designer: Rosie Bellwood

ISBN: 978-1-3988-4327-1
CH011577NT
Supplier 29, Date 0824, PI 00006502

Printed in China

CONTENTS

INTRODUCTION
RENAISSANCE MAN

Leonardo da Vinci (1452–1519) was a man of many talents. Not only was he one of the greatest artists in history, he was also a brilliant scientist, architect, writer, musician, engineer, and inventor. Today, he is regarded as one of the most gifted and intelligent people who ever lived.

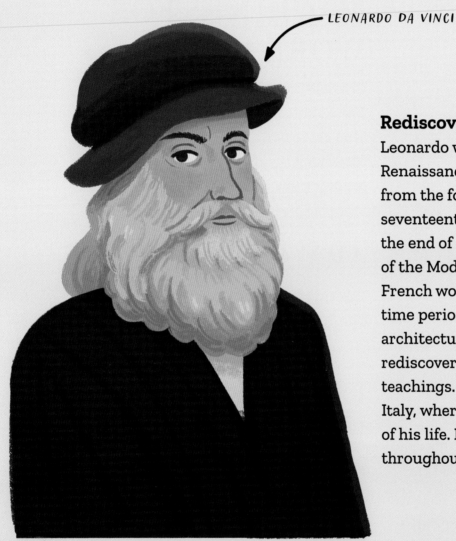

LEONARDO DA VINCI

Rediscovery of Learning

Leonardo was a leading figure of the Renaissance, an era in European history from the fourteenth century to the seventeenth century. This period marked the end of the Middle Ages and the start of the Modern Era. "Renaissance" is a French word meaning "rebirth." This time period saw a revival of science, art, architecture, and music, inspired by the rediscovery of ancient Greek and Roman teachings. The Renaissance began in Italy, where Leonardo spent almost all of his life. Later, the movement spread throughout the rest of Europe.

Humans at the Heart

At the heart of the Renaissance was a movement known as humanism, which placed humans at the heart of the universe. Humanists believed there was no limit to human development and that people should embrace knowledge and develop their talents as fully as possible. Those who strove to develop skills in many different areas have become known as Renaissance men. Leonardo was one of the foremost examples of a Renaissance man.

A Man of Many Talents

While he was alive, and for centuries afterward, Leonardo was known mainly for his art, especially for his world-famous paintings the *Mona Lisa* and *The Last Supper*. But Leonardo was far more than an artist. During his life, he produced thousands of pages of notes on a vast range of scientific topics. These notes only came to widespread public attention in the nineteenth century. Today, Leonardo is revered as a scientist as much as he is an artist.

LEONARDO'S NOTEBOOKS

Leonardo the Inventor

In his notes, Leonardo also jotted down ideas for some spectacular inventions that were far ahead of their time. In this book, we will mainly focus on Leonardo's genius as an inventor.

TECHNOLOGY IN LEONARDO'S TIME

One reason Leonardo did not achieve fame as an inventor while he was alive was because he was so far ahead of his time—literally. The tools and technologies needed to build his inventions did not yet exist in the fifteenth and sixteenth centuries, and they would not exist for several hundred more years.

Imagining a Future World

In his notes and sketches, Leonardo dreamed up a world of cars, planes, helicopters, scuba divers, submarines, robots, and tanks. In a sense, he invented the twentieth century! Yet many of his ideas were impractical and never got beyond the drawing board. This was often because they required a different kind of energy to power them than what was available during Leonardo's lifetime.

Energy Source Limitations

In Leonardo's day, sources of energy were limited, and humans still relied on muscle power to build structures, carry loads, and grow crops. Horses, mules, and oxen helped to transport people and goods in carts. Animals were also used to turn treadmills to raise water, or to lift heavy weights.

A HORSE AND CART

Fire, Wind, and Water Energy

Firewood and charcoal provided another energy source—fire—for warmth and cooking. Wind energy propelled sailing ships across the sea, and provided rotational power to windmills for pumping water and grinding corn. Flowing rivers drove waterwheels to power various industrial activities such as grinding grain, sawing timber, or making paper and fabric.

Ahead of the Time

Many of Leonardo's inventions would have required more powerful, mobile, and efficient energy sources than fire, wind, and water. In the eighteenth and nineteenth centuries, inventions like the steam engine, electric motor, and internal combustion engine were more powerful and mobile. If steam, electric, and liquid fuel power had been available to Leonardo, he could have turned his fantastical ideas into real working machines!

LEONARDO'S LIFE
STUDIO BOY

Leonardo da Vinci was born on April 15th, 1452, near the small town of Vinci, not far from Florence. His father was Piero da Vinci, a lawyer. His mother, Caterina di Meo Lippi, was a peasant woman. His parents were not married when Leonardo was born, and they both went on to marry other people.

Early Years

Little is known about Leonardo's childhood or where he lived. Since his parents were unmarried at the time of his birth, it is unlikely he lived with his father in Florence. It's believed that he lived his first years with his mother in Vinci and then went to live with his paternal grandfather, Antonio da Vinci, by the age of five. Leonardo's humble beginnings meant he only received a basic education in reading, writing, and mathematics, according to the social customs of the day.

LEONARDO AS A BOY

ANDREA DEL VERROCCHIO

Enthusiastic Apprentice

When he was about fourteen, Leonardo's family moved to Florence. He must have shown some artistic promise because, thanks to his father's connections, he was offered a job as a studio boy in the workshop of Andrea del Verrocchio—the leading painter and sculptor in Florence at the time. At the age of seventeen, Leonardo became Verrocchio's apprentice.

Outstanding Talent

The apprentices in Verrocchio's studio did many of the paintings. Leonardo was surrounded by highly talented men who would have taught him many valuable artistic skills, including drawing, painting, sculpting, metalwork, plaster casting, mechanics, and woodwork. In time, Leonardo's talent began to attract outside attention. According to one story, he painted a monster on a shield that was so impressive, the Duke of Milan bought it.

RENAISSANCE ARTIST'S STUDIO

Promising Artist

In 1472, Leonardo was accepted into the Painters' Guild of Florence, yet he remained with Verrocchio for five further years. Afterward, he established himself as an independent painter in a workshop in Florence. Many of his works from this period were sketches of military weapons and machines, demonstrating his interest in technology even at this early stage of his career.

ARTIST AND ENGINEER

In 1482, Leonardo moved to Milan to work for the city's duke, Ludovico Sforza. By this time, Leonardo had become known as a man of many talents. The duke kept him busy as a painter, sculptor, and designer of court festivals. Sforza also frequently consulted Leonardo on matters of architecture, military fortifications, and engineering projects.

LEONARDO SHOWING HIS PLANS TO THE DUKE OF MILAN

Milan

While in Milan, Leonardo created a number of famous works. From 1483 to 1486, he worked on the altar painting *The Virgin of the Rocks*. From 1495 to 1498, he worked on *The Last Supper*, which he painted on a wall in the monastery of Santa Maria delle Grazie. To commemorate the duke's father, Francesco Sforza, Leonardo spent twelve years creating an enormous horse statue that stood 5 m high (16 ft). He first completed a clay model of the statue and made preparations to cast it in bronze. But due to the looming threat of war, the metal was used to make cannons instead.

On to Venice

In 1499, the French invaded Milan and Ludovico fell from power. Leonardo left the city shortly afterward and moved to Venice, where he was employed as a military architect and engineer, devising machines to defend the city from naval attack. In 1502, Leonardo entered the service of Cesare Borgia, a powerful duke who commissioned him to create a map of the city of Imola. Leonardo's map was so accurate, it can still be used to navigate the city today!

HOW LEONARDO'S HORSE STATUE WOULD HAVE LOOKED

LEONARDO PAINTING THE MONA LISA

Back to Florence

Returning to his home city of Florence in 1503, Leonardo was given a hero's welcome. He was immediately commissioned to create a huge mural, entitled *Battle of Anghiari*, for Florence's Palazzo Vecchio. He worked on it for three years, but never completed it. He also embarked on his most famous painting, the *Mona Lisa*, which he would continue working on into old age. In his spare time, the ever-restless Leonardo pursued his own scientific studies—investigating human anatomy, the flight of birds, and hydrology (the study of water).

LATER YEARS

Leonardo returned to Milan in 1506 and went to work for the city's French governor Charles d'Amboise. He did not paint much during this period and spent most of his time advising Charles on architectural matters, while continuing his studies in science, mathematics, optics, geology, and botany.

GIULIANO DE' MEDICI

Rome

In 1513, political turmoil in Milan forced Leonardo to move once again. This time he went to Rome, where he entered into the service of Giuliano de' Medici, brother of Pope Leo X. Giuliano gave Leonardo a suite of rooms in the Vatican and a monthly allowance.

This was a time of great artistic activity for artists such as Raphael and Michelangelo, who were both busy with projects for the Pope. Leonardo was not offered any major art commissions, but he remained busy with his scientific work, dissecting corpses and studying botany in the Vatican gardens. In 1514, Giuliano ordered the draining of the Pontine Marshes, and Leonardo created an impressive map of the area. He also made sketches for a new palace in Florence for the Medici family, but it was never built.

France

In 1516, King Francis I of France invited Leonardo to enter into his service. At the age of sixty-five, Leonardo left Italy. It was his first and only trip outside his home country—and it would also be his last. He settled with Francesco Melzi, his most devoted pupil, in the Manoir du Cloux (now called Clos Lucé)—a large château near the king's summer palace of Amboise on the River Loire.

LEONARDO DRAWING A MAP OF THE PONTINE MARSHES

The King's Friend

King Francis treated Leonardo with the greatest respect, and the two became close friends. Leonardo was granted the title of "First painter, architect, and engineer to the King," and was given complete freedom. He did little painting in France, although he did create a series of dramatic drawings depicting the elemental forces of nature, called *Visions of the End of the World.* Most of his time was spent collecting and editing his scientific papers. He also drew up plans for a palace and garden for the king's mother, and he built a mechanical lion for a court festival. Leonardo died at his home in 1519, aged sixty-seven, possibly of a stroke.

MANOIR DU CLOUX

As a well-spent day brings happy sleep, so life well used brings happy death.
Leonardo da Vinci, *The Notebooks of Leonardo da Vinci.*

THE NOTEBOOKS

In the early 1480s, Leonardo began writing his thoughts down on paper. He wrote and sketched almost every day, making continual observations of the world around him. In total, he produced some 13,000 densely written pages on the topics of science, engineering, and art.

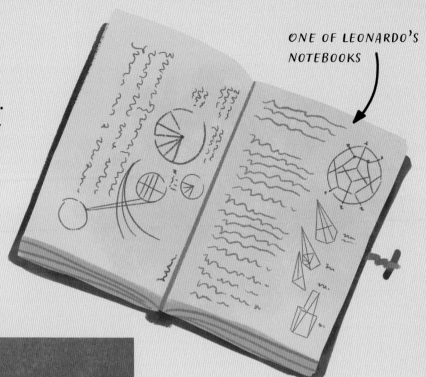

ONE OF LEONARDO'S NOTEBOOKS

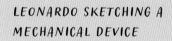

LEONARDO SKETCHING A MECHANICAL DEVICE

Many Interests

Leonardo's notes revealed his wide range of interests. They contained scientific observations and theories, designs for exotic machines, sketches for future paintings, studies of faces and emotions, designs for buildings, human anatomy, rock formations, and whirlpools. They also contained mundane items such as shopping lists and the names of people who owed him money.

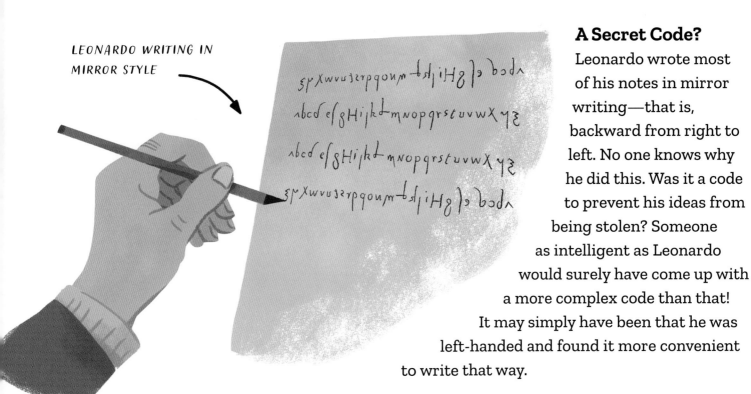

A Secret Code?

Leonardo wrote most of his notes in mirror writing—that is, backward from right to left. No one knows why he did this. Was it a code to prevent his ideas from being stolen? Someone as intelligent as Leonardo would surely have come up with a more complex code than that! It may simply have been that he was left-handed and found it more convenient to write that way.

Forgotten Treasure

Leonardo always hoped his notes would be published one day. When he died, the notebooks were given to his pupil Francesco Melzi, who did little with them. Melzi may have been daunted by the challenge. After all, there were thousands of pages on many diverse subjects, arranged in no particular order. After Melzi's death in 1570, the collection passed to his son Orazio, who put them in his attic and forgot about them.

FRANCESCO MELZI

Rediscovered and Revered

In the seventeenth century, renewed interest in Leonardo's notes began to spread. By this time, many of them had been bound into volumes, and had found their way into art collections. Others had been lost to time. It was only in the 1800s that scholars began studying the notebooks. Today, Leonardo's surviving notebooks— consisting of around 7,000 pages—are housed in libraries and museums in Italy, France, Spain, the UK, and the USA. One is owned by American tech pioneer and philanthropist Bill Gates. Efforts were made to translate the notebooks and they are available online.

THE SCIENCE OF MACHINES

Leonardo's machines may have been great feats of the imagination, but they were not works of fantasy. His ideas were based on real mechanical and scientific principles. Many of them have been built—and shown to work—by modern engineers. Where did Leonardo acquire his knowledge and expertise?

Tapping Ancient Knowledge

Much of Leonardo's understanding of science and technology came from ancient Greek and medieval "natural philosophers" (an old term for scientists), including Aristotle (384–322 BCE) and Archimedes (287–212 BCE). Leonardo learned about motion and equilibrium (in which opposing forces are balanced). He also studied simple machines and machine parts: levers, wedges, pulleys, screws, inclined planes, and the wheel and axle.

THE SIX SIMPLE MACHINES

Hero of Alexandria (first century CE) was the first to write about gears: devices that transfer power from one part of a machine to another. In about 530 CE, John Philoponus developed the concept of momentum.

A SET OF GEARS

Learning by Doing

Leonardo did not solely rely on the wisdom of the ancients. He also learned a great deal through his own observations and experiments. This approach was innovative at a time when most people learned about natural philosophy simply by reading. Leonardo's research led him to make several key scientific discoveries. For example, he discovered the laws of friction by sliding heavy objects down inclined planes, and he made breakthroughs in the science of flight by studying birds. Leonardo was also a pioneer in the study of materials, motion, vacuums, and water pressure. He discovered principles that would later be rediscovered by scientists such as Galileo, Newton, and Coulomb.

Motion

Pushing Force

Friction

Perpetual Motion

In Leonardo's perpetual motion machine, the weight of the ball bearings should, in theory, keep the wheel turning forever. After much study, Leonardo concluded that perpetual motion was impossible.

From Mind to Machine

Leonardo used his knowledge of science and engineering to design machines that the world had never before seen or imagined—machines that foretold the technological future. Let's take a look at some of these inventions of a genius!

AIR AND WATER MACHINES
THE FLYING MACHINE

Leonardo was fascinated by the possibility of human flight. He produced more than 35,000 words and five hundred sketches on the subject of flying machines, the nature of air, and bird flight. He believed that humans could, with the right technology, imitate the flight of winged animals. One of his most famous inventions, designed in the 1490s, was the flying machine, or ornithopter.

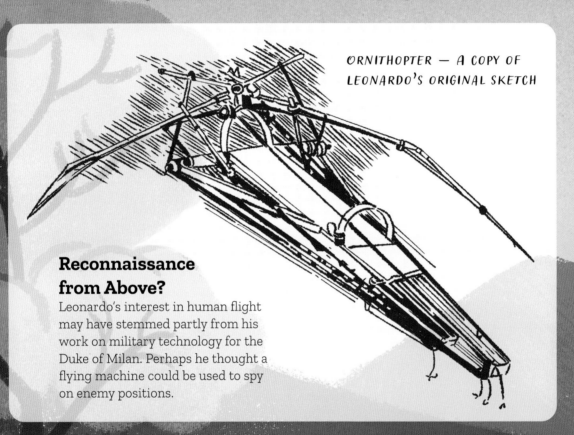

ORNITHOPTER — A COPY OF LEONARDO'S ORIGINAL SKETCH

Reconnaissance from Above?
Leonardo's interest in human flight may have stemmed partly from his work on military technology for the Duke of Milan. Perhaps he thought a flying machine could be used to spy on enemy positions.

How Did it Work?
The Ornithopter consisted of a pair of giant wings, with a total span of around 10 m (33 ft), and a narrow board between them where the pilot would lie face down. The wings consisted of a lightweight pine wood frame covered in a membrane (skin) of raw silk.

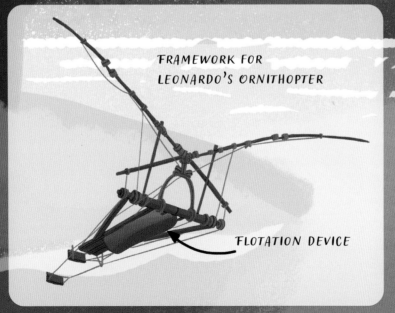

FRAMEWORK FOR LEONARDO'S ORNITHOPTER

FLOTATION DEVICE

Leonardo understood that human arms alone lacked the strength to lift the structure into the air. So he added a pair of pedals so the pilot could use foot power. The pedals moved a series of rods and pulleys connected to the wings. One raised the wings; the other lowered them. The pilot would rotate a crank with his hands to provide additional power. A headpiece operated a rudder to steer the craft. The wings were designed to rotate as they flapped, much like the wings of birds.

Safety Concerns

For safety reasons, Leonardo recommended that the ornithopter be tested over a body of water. He added an air-filled flotation device beneath the pilot's board—just in case.

Could it Fly?

Try as he might, Leonardo never overcame the problem that human muscle power is insufficient to generate both lift and propulsion. The ornithopter might have flown once it was up in the air, but the pilot would not have been able to flap the wings fast enough to get it off the ground. Legend has it that Leonardo and an assistant tested the flying machine on Monte Ceceri, a hill near Florence, but there is no evidence to suggest this actually happened.

Since the wings are swifter to press the air than the air is to escape from beneath the wings, the air becomes condensed and resists the movement of the wings.
Leonardo da Vinci, *The Notebooks of Leonardo da Vinci* (1938).

THE AERIAL SCREW

In the late 1480s, Leonardo drew a sketch of a flying machine that had similarities to a modern helicopter. The aircraft had a large blade that would rotate in a spiral, giving it lift and propulsion. The aerial screw was a forerunner of the screw propeller on ships, except it was designed to push against air rather than water.

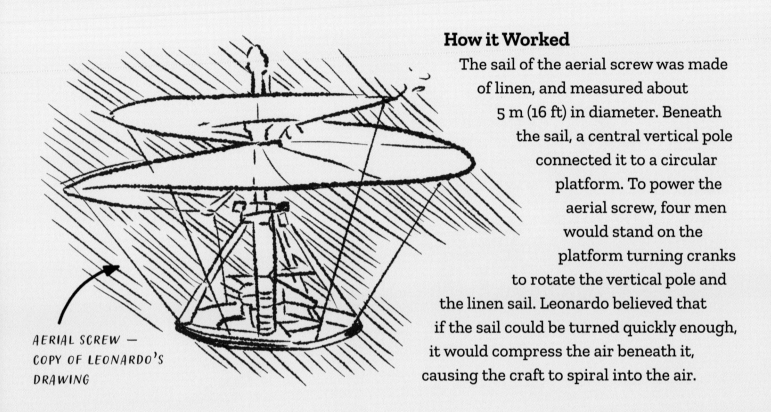

AERIAL SCREW —
COPY OF LEONARDO'S
DRAWING

How it Worked

The sail of the aerial screw was made of linen, and measured about 5 m (16 ft) in diameter. Beneath the sail, a central vertical pole connected it to a circular platform. To power the aerial screw, four men would stand on the platform turning cranks to rotate the vertical pole and the linen sail. Leonardo believed that if the sail could be turned quickly enough, it would compress the air beneath it, causing the craft to spiral into the air.

Could it Have Flown?

There is no evidence that Leonardo ever tried building the aerial screw, though he may have produced some small working models. Modern scientists believe the machine would have been too heavy to fly. The four men turning the cranks would not have been able to generate enough power to overcome gravity. Also, the spinning of the sail may have caused the platform to rotate in the opposite direction—a dizzying experience for those on board. In 2022, an engineering team at the University of Maryland, USA, designed a drone based on Leonardo's aerial screw, and it flew!

AERIAL SCREW — HOW IT WOULD HAVE LOOKED IN REALITY

Did Leonardo Invent the Helicopter?

Leonardo's idea that a spinning blade can compress the air beneath it to generate lift was correct, and is the principle behind modern helicopters. What he lacked was an engine powerful enough to give the machine lift-off. Still, Leonardo's invention is regarded as the world's first idea for a vertical flying machine.

THE MEN PUSH THE CRANK, MOVING IN THE SAME DIRECTION AS THE SAIL AS IT STARTS TO TURN.

AERIAL SCREW — THE TWO WAYS IT COULD HAVE WORKED

Inspired by Nature

Unlike most early flying machine designs, the aerial screw did not have any bird-like features. The screw shape may have been inspired by Leonardo's observations of spinning maple or sycamore seed pods as they fell to the ground.

THE MEN PUSH WITH THEIR FEET AGAINST THE BASE, MAKING THE SAIL TURN IN THE OPPOSITE DIRECTION.

THE PARACHUTE

In December 1783, French scientist and monk Louis-Sébastien Lenormand made the first recorded descent in a parachute, jumping from the tower of Montpellier observatory. The origins of the parachute go back a lot further, though. The earliest design appeared in the 1470s in an anonymous Italian manuscript. It showed a man hanging from a cone-shaped canopy, which was intended as an escape device to allow people to jump from burning buildings. A few years later, around 1483, Leonardo da Vinci sketched his own, more sophisticated parachute design.

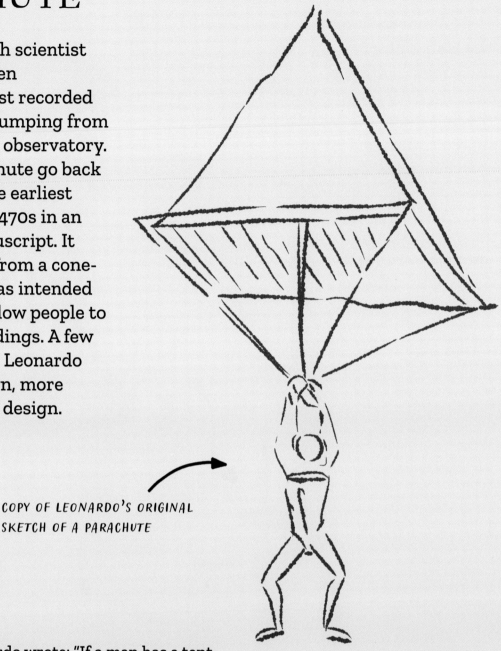

COPY OF LEONARDO'S ORIGINAL SKETCH OF A PARACHUTE

Leonardo's Tent

Next to his sketch, Leonardo wrote: "If a man has a tent made of linen of which the apertures [openings] have all been stopped up, and it be twelve bracchia [7 m / 23 ft] across and twelve in depth, he will be able to throw himself down from any great height without suffering any injury." Leonardo had clearly thought about the size the parachute would need to be in order to hold the weight of the jumper. The sealed linen cloth would be attached to a pyramid-shaped frame of wooden poles, and would be opened by the person as they fell. The air trapped within the canopy would slow their descent, allowing them to land safely.

Putting the Parachute to the Test

Like many of Leonardo's inventions, there is no evidence that he ever built or tested his parachute. Some scientists suspect the wooden frame would have been too heavy and the canopy too weak to land someone safely. In 2000, a British man named Adrian Nichols decided to test it out. He constructed a parachute based on Leonardo's design, using the canvas and timber that would have been available during Leonardo's time. He even used tools from the Renaissance era to build it.

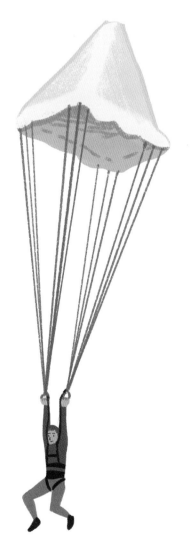

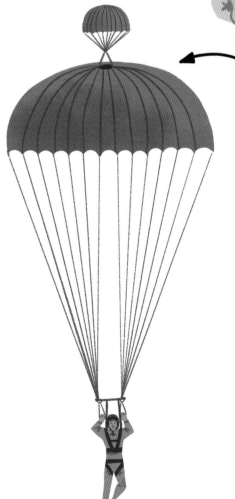

ADRIAN NICHOLS' VERSION OF LEONARDO'S PARACHUTE NEXT TO A MODERN DESIGN

Nichols dropped from a hot-air balloon 3,000 m (9,842 ft) above the open spaces of Mpumalanga, South Africa. To ensure the heavy device did not crash down on top of him on landing, he cut himself free at 600 m (1,969 ft) and deployed a second, modern parachute. Leonardo's parachute worked beautifully! Nichols said the ride was smoother than that of a modern parachute.

ANEMOMETER

Leonardo's interest in flight may have inspired him to create his anemometer—an instrument for measuring wind speed. Perhaps he hoped his device would help future aviators before they attempted take off. His was not the first anemometer. Another Italian Renaissance man, Leon Battista Alberti, came up with a design in 1450. However, Leonardo's version, created some time between 1483 and 1486, was more accurate and easier to use.

Leonardo's Harp

Alberti's design consisted of a flat plate suspended from the top. The wind would cause the plate to twist, and the wind's force could be measured by how far it twisted. Leonardo's anemometer had an arched frame with a rectangular block of wood hanging in the middle by a hinge. When the wind blew, it raised the piece of wood within the arched frame. Printed on the inside of the frame was a scale. By noting the point the wood reached on the scale, a person could measure the force of the wind. Not only was Leonardo's anemometer practical, it was also beautiful—its shape was similar to that of a harp, perhaps reflecting his love of music.

LEONARDO'S ANEMOMETER

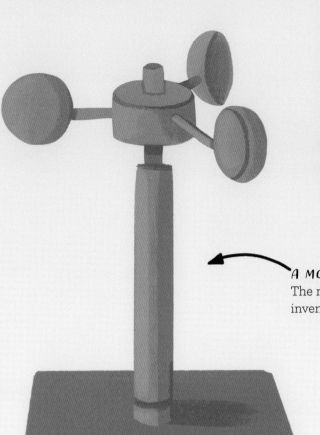

Clocking Speed

Next to his sketch of the anemometer, Leonardo wrote: "For measuring distance traversed per hour with the force of the wind, here a clock for showing time is required." By adding a clock to his device, wind-speed records could be made at regular time intervals, giving a useful gauge of average wind speeds over a period of time.

A MODERN ANEMOMETER
The modern hemispherical cup anemometer was invented by John Robinson in 1846.

Beeswax and Cotton

In 1480, Leonardo sketched another device for measuring the weather—the hygrometer, which measures the degree of humidity (moisture) in the air. Based on an idea by German philosopher Nicholas of Cusa, Leonardo's design consisted of a weight scale with two pans. In one pan was a piece of beeswax, which does not change in moist conditions. In the other was a cotton ball. As the cotton absorbed moisture, it tipped the scales. A measuring stick marked the exact increase in its weight and therefore the amount of moisture in the air.

HYGROMETER

THE DIVING SUIT

In 1500, Leonardo was living in Venice, the "water city." At that time, Venice was under attack by the Ottoman Empire's navy. The city needed help, and Leonardo responded with a design for an underwater diving suit. His idea was that divers could conduct surprise attacks on enemy ships entering Venetian waters. This was a far-fetched notion in Leonardo's day, and shows once more his unique ability to anticipate the future of technology.

LEONARDO'S DIVING SUIT

Leather, Fish Oil, and Glass

The device consisted of a pigskin leather suit treated with fish oil to repel water, and a bag-like face mask including glass goggles. The mask was equipped with a valve-operated goatskin balloon that could be inflated or deflated to help the diver rise or sink. The air supply came via two hollow breathing tubes made of cane, with pigskin joints and reinforced with steel rings to resist water pressure. These led from the diver's mouth to a cork diving bell floating on the surface. The suit even contained a special "pee pouch," so the diver did not have to return to the surface to relieve himself!

Testing the Suit

A replica of the suit was constructed for a 2003 documentary about Leonardo's drawings and notes. Its appearance was alarming—it looked like some kind of swamp monster! But when scuba divers tested it, they found that it worked well.

Submarine

Leonardo also proposed an idea for a submarine. Worried the plan might fall into enemy hands, he drew it disassembled (in separate parts) and made it deliberately difficult to understand. The submarine would be taken, by ship, to a place close to an enemy vessel, then would be lowered by a rope-and-pulley system into the water. It had two air chambers for breathing. To propel the craft, the pilot would turn a set of foot pedals, activating two fins at the rear. A pair of hand-operated rudders were used for steering. Once at the target, the submarine had a set of spring and screw weapons to pierce the enemy ship's hull.

SUBMARINE

BRIDGES

During his time in Milan in the 1480s, Leonardo advised Duke Ludovico Sforza on various military engineering projects. One idea he came up with was for a swing bridge. Marching armies needed to build bridges to cross rivers and streams, but they didn't want these bridges to be used by the enemy later, so they often resorted to destroying them. The swing bridge offered a less wasteful solution: it could be swung away from the river once the army had crossed it, so the enemy could not follow.

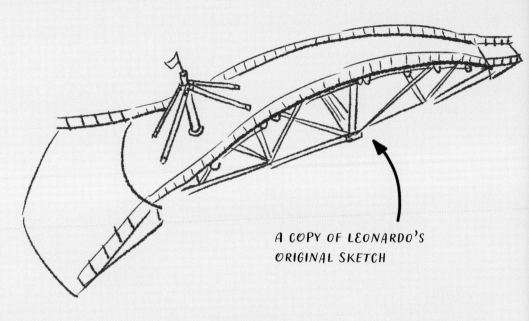

A COPY OF LEONARDO'S ORIGINAL SKETCH

Portable Bridge

The single-span bridge would be fixed to one of the banks by a vertical post acting as a pivot, allowing it to rotate. Using a rope-and-pulley system of cords, wheels, and winches, the bridge could be turned 90 degrees away from the opposite river bank. To prevent the bridge from collapsing under its own weight while being opened, Leonardo added a tank filled with stones to act as a counterbalance. The bridge had a simple, lightweight construction and could be packed up quickly and transported for use elsewhere.

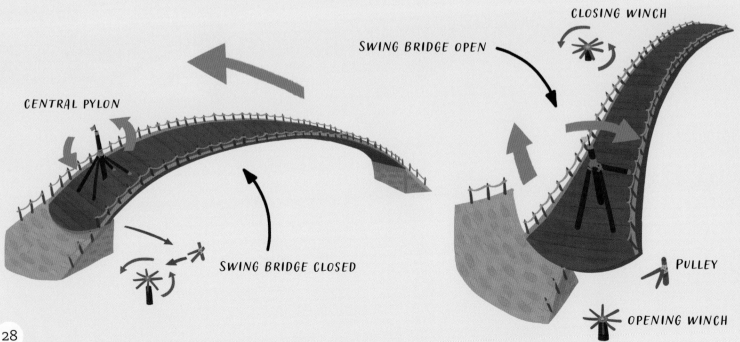

CLOSING WINCH

SWING BRIDGE OPEN

CENTRAL PYLON

SWING BRIDGE CLOSED

PULLEY

OPENING WINCH

The Sultan's Bridge

In 1502, Sultan Bayezid II, ruler of the Ottoman Empire, requested proposals for a bridge to connect Istanbul with the nearby citadel of Galata. Leonardo came up with a design, which he described in a letter to the Sultan. Instead of a row of piers and semi-circular arches—the standard bridge design of the time—he proposed a single flattened arch to cross the entire span. The bridge would have been around 280 m (919 ft) long, making it the world's longest single-span bridge at that time. Leonardo included abutments (structure supports) that splayed outward on either side to support it against lateral (sideways) motions in this earthquake-prone region.

SULTAN'S BRIDGE

Testing the Structure

Sadly, the sultan rejected the design, but in 2019, engineers at the Massachusetts Institute of Technology (MIT) built a scale model of the bridge using 3D printing, and proved that the bridge would have worked. The structure gave it an internal stability that ensured it would not topple.

WATER MACHINES

Leonardo spent decades of his life studying water—the way it moved and flowed—and dreamed up ways that people could work with it. He was the first to propose turning the Arno River into a navigable canal between Florence and Pisa, and he invented a canal lock that is still in use today. He also devised machines for lifting water, creating fountains and whirlpools, and for draining ponds and swamps.

"Water is the vehicle of nature."
Leonardo da Vinci

Centrifuge

Leonardo designed a centrifuge (a rapidly rotating container) as a drainage machine. It would be turned by flowing river water, or mounted on a boat and turned by animals. This would form whirlpools that would suck up the water.

HYDRAULIC SAW

Water-powered Saw

One of Leonardo's hydraulic (water-powered) designs was for a mechanical saw. A channel of flowing river water would turn a waterwheel, which would rotate an axle. A crankshaft would then convert this rotary motion into reciprocating (up-down) motion to drive the saw blade. The mechanism would simultaneously work a system of pulleys to pull a log through the cutting blade.

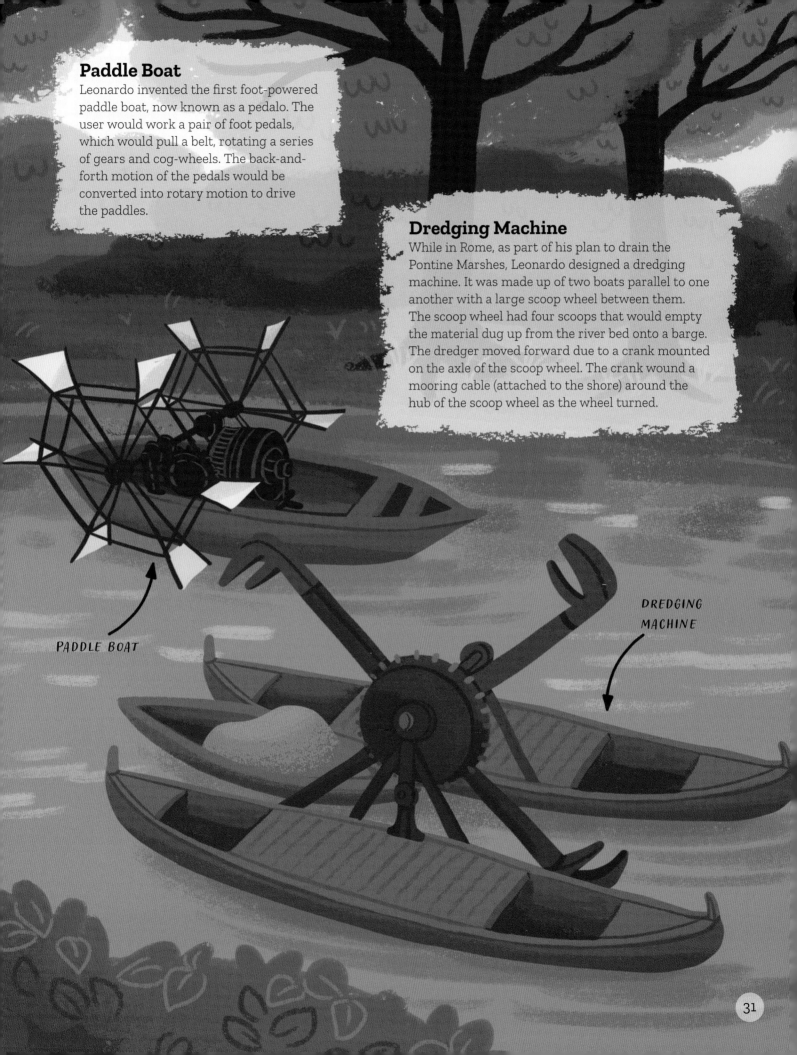

Paddle Boat

Leonardo invented the first foot-powered paddle boat, now known as a pedalo. The user would work a pair of foot pedals, which would pull a belt, rotating a series of gears and cog-wheels. The back-and-forth motion of the pedals would be converted into rotary motion to drive the paddles.

Dredging Machine

While in Rome, as part of his plan to drain the Pontine Marshes, Leonardo designed a dredging machine. It was made up of two boats parallel to one another with a large scoop wheel between them. The scoop wheel had four scoops that would empty the material dug up from the river bed onto a barge. The dredger moved forward due to a crank mounted on the axle of the scoop wheel. The crank wound a mooring cable (attached to the shore) around the hub of the scoop wheel as the wheel turned.

PADDLE BOAT

DREDGING MACHINE

WAR MACHINES
THE GIANT CROSSBOW

Throughout much of Leonardo's life, the Italian peninsula was plagued by warfare. His patrons were always interested in new ideas for weapons to give them an advantage over their enemies. Leonardo obliged with a number of innovative designs. One of the most spectacular of these was his giant crossbow. He presented this in 1488–89 to his employer, Duke Ludovico Sforza of Milan.

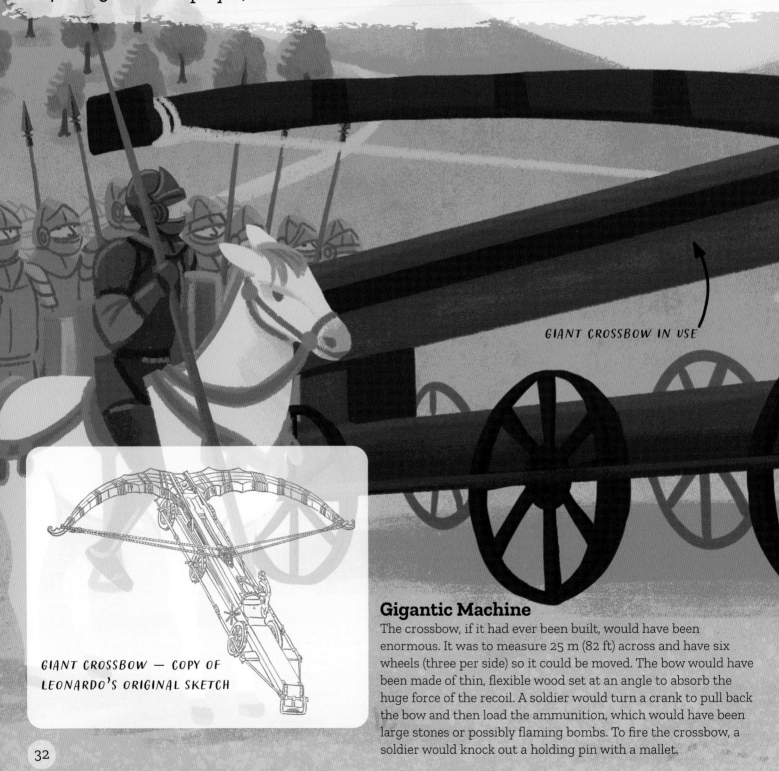

GIANT CROSSBOW IN USE

GIANT CROSSBOW — COPY OF LEONARDO'S ORIGINAL SKETCH

Gigantic Machine

The crossbow, if it had ever been built, would have been enormous. It was to measure 25 m (82 ft) across and have six wheels (three per side) so it could be moved. The bow would have been made of thin, flexible wood set at an angle to absorb the huge force of the recoil. A soldier would turn a crank to pull back the bow and then load the ammunition, which would have been large stones or possibly flaming bombs. To fire the crossbow, a soldier would knock out a holding pin with a mallet.

To Scare and Intimidate

The giant crossbow was designed as a siege weapon, much like a catapult, hurling stones at the walls of castles and citadels. However, Leonardo may have intended it mainly to stoke fear in the enemy and to deter them from attacking. There is no record of it ever being built—it may have been beyond the technology of the time. However, a working replica of the giant crossbow was constructed in 2003 for a British documentary called *Leonardo's Dream Machines*.

Rapid-firing Crossbow

Leonardo had another idea for a rapid-firing crossbow that would have been powered by a huge treadmill turned by several strong men treading steps around the wheel's rim. It would have featured four crossbows, and as it rotated, a system of interconnected gears, pulleys, and ropes would have loaded arrows ready to fire. The men on the treadmill would have been hidden behind a protective wooden shield.

RAPID-FIRING CROSSBOW

THE MULTI-BARREL CANNON

Gunpowder started to change warfare in Leonardo's day, but cannons were heavy, static weapons, slow to reload after each round of firing. In 1480, Leonardo offered a way around this problem with his design for a multi-barrel cannon. Not only did it drastically reduce reloading times, it could also be moved quickly and easily.

MULTI-BARREL
CANNON — COPY
OF LEONARDO'S
ORIGINAL SKETCHES

Devastating Weapon

The multi-barrel cannon had eleven thin barrels. While one barrel was fired, other barrels could be loaded, increasing the frequency of fire. The barrels were arranged in a fan-like shape that widened the field of fire, making it especially deadly against advancing troops. Ammunition was loaded from the rear (breech loading), unlike the more common muzzle-loaded cannons of the time. This cut down the time it took to reload the machine.

Mobility

Despite the number of barrels, Leonardo designed his weapon to be lightweight. It sat on a gun carriage with large wheels, making it easy to move on the battlefield. The carriage was easily lifted and turned to fire in different directions. The angle of the barrels could be adjusted by turning a crank on the rear of the carriage, which impacted the range of fire.

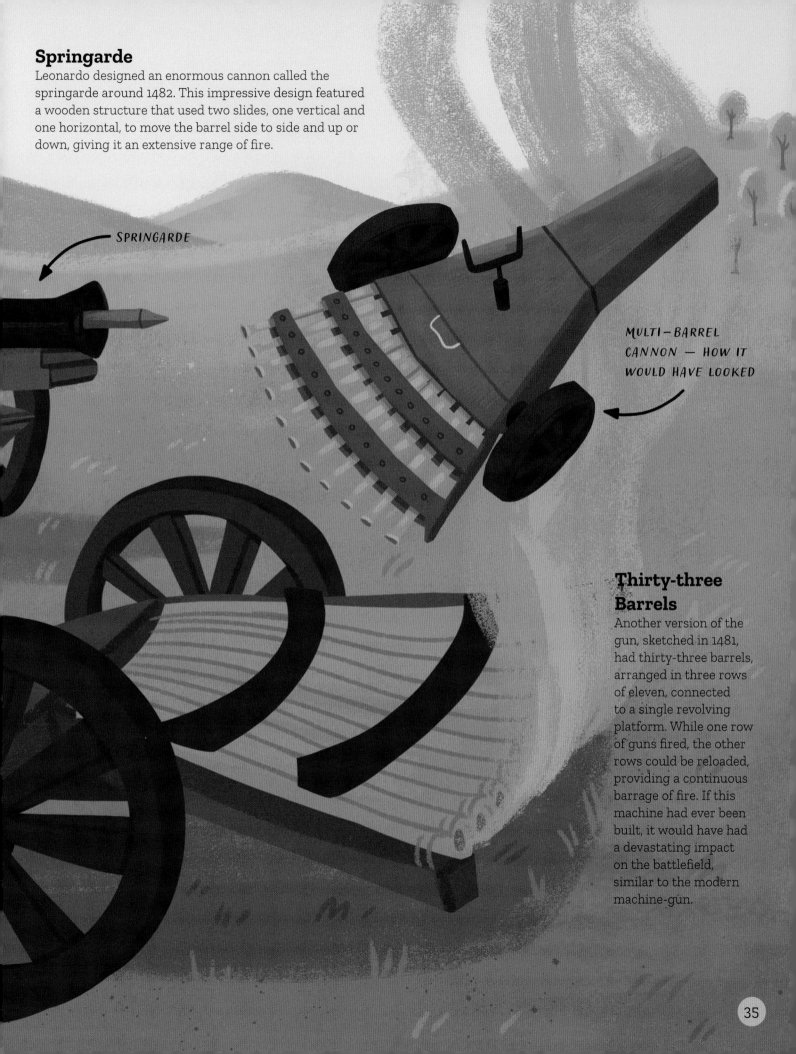

Springarde

Leonardo designed an enormous cannon called the springarde around 1482. This impressive design featured a wooden structure that used two slides, one vertical and one horizontal, to move the barrel side to side and up or down, giving it an extensive range of fire.

SPRINGARDE

MULTI—BARREL CANNON — HOW IT WOULD HAVE LOOKED

Thirty-three Barrels

Another version of the gun, sketched in 1481, had thirty-three barrels, arranged in three rows of eleven, connected to a single revolving platform. While one row of guns fired, the other rows could be reloaded, providing a continuous barrage of fire. If this machine had ever been built, it would have had a devastating impact on the battlefield, similar to the modern machine-gun.

EARLY TANK

In 1487, Leonardo wrote to Duke Sforza of Milan explaining that he could make a tank that could "enter the close ranks of the enemy and break through any company of soldiers." Leonardo's design was a forerunner of today's tank—a vehicle that could move through the battlefield causing destruction while keeping its crew protected.

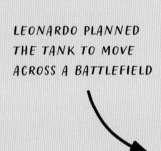

LEONARDO PLANNED THE TANK TO MOVE ACROSS A BATTLEFIELD

TURTLE
The turtle, with its upper and lower carapace, inspired Leonardo's design for a tank.

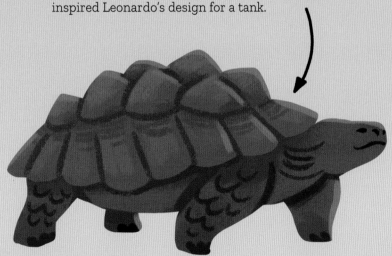

Protective Shell

The vehicle would have been fitted with thirty-six light cannons, arranged around the perimeter of a circular platform, allowing shots to be fired in any direction. The platform would have been enclosed by a protective covering of wood reinforced with metal plates. Its slanted angles would deflect enemy fire, much like the tanks of World War II. A turret at the top enabled a lookout to coordinate firing and steering.

A Turtle's Pace

Four men turned cranks in the middle of the platform to set the wheels in motion. How could they move such a heavy machine? It may have been possible due to the gear ratios of the mechanism, but the vehicle would have moved very slowly (like going in first gear on a bike up a hill—exerting lots of effort for a slow speed). Leonardo considered using horses for power, but decided against it because the animals may have panicked inside the confined space, especially during battle.

CUTAWAY TO SHOW TANK INTERIOR

Imperfect Design

Surprisingly, Leonardo's design contained a major flaw. The cranks that powered the tank went in opposite directions, making forward motion impossible. Scholars have debated how a detail-oriented genius like Leonardo could have made such a basic error. Some suggest he was a pacifist at heart and deliberately sabotaged his design to ensure it would never work. Others have said it was a security measure in case the enemy ever got hold of it. And there was another problem—on the muddy, uneven terrain of battlefields, its wheels would have become stuck. Leonardo added studs to the wheels for traction, but this would be of little help in muddy conditions. Modern tanks overcame this issue with caterpillar tracks.

MARCHING DRUM

In Leonardo's day, soldiers would march into battle accompanied by the rhythmic sound of drums. Drummers were vulnerable, and many were killed in battle. Leonardo reasoned that a mechanical drum, pulled by one man, might produce a sound loud enough to replace a dozen individual drummers, potentially saving lives.

How it Worked

The mechanical drum, designed around 1489–92, took the form of a cart pulled by a person.

1. As the wheels turned, they rotated a toothed wheel attached to the axle.

2. The toothed wheel engaged with a cage-shaped gear at the base of a pair of cylinders, causing them to rotate.

3. The cylinders had holes in them where pegs could be inserted.

4. These pegs activated the spring-powered drumsticks—five on each side—that then rhythmically struck the drum.

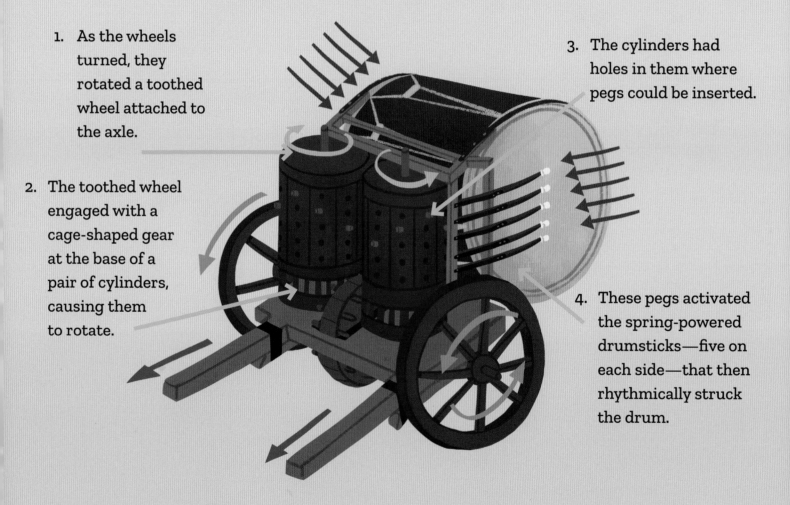

The operator would only need to keep the speed of the cart constant to maintain a steady rhythm. The drum would have been large enough to make an ominous booming sound during battle.

Programmable Rhythms

The most fascinating part of this device was that it could be programmed. The pegs inserted in the two cylinders could be placed in different holes, producing different beat sequences and rhythms. For a steady beat, the pegs would need to be placed in a straight line—vertically for a slow beat or diagonally for a fast one. Any variation from this would produce more complex rhythms. If the pegs on both cylinders were in the same equivalent position, they would strike the drum simultaneously on both sides to produce a louder sound, amplifying certain beats in the rhythm. As an accomplished musician, Leonardo would likely have been interested in this aspect of his design.

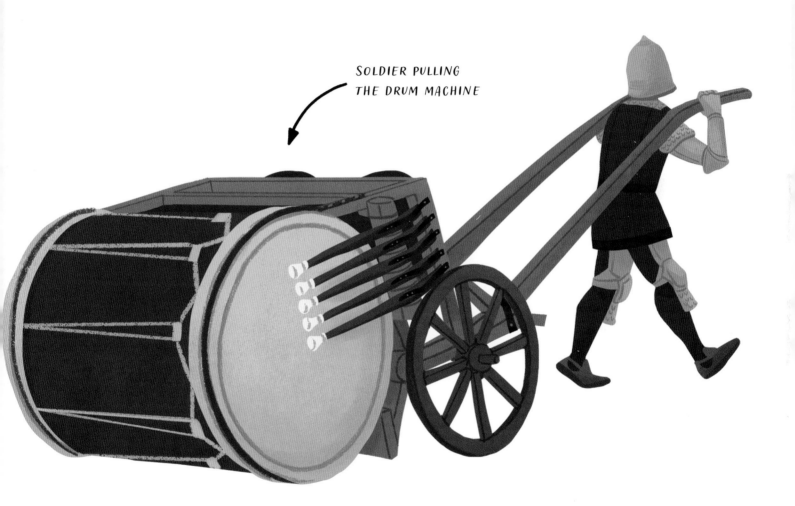

SOLDIER PULLING THE DRUM MACHINE

Drumming in Place

Leonardo also provided a version of the drum for parades or areas where movement was limited. In this case, the machine was activated not by the movement of the wheels, but by a hand crank.

Duplicate Drum

A replica of Leonardo's mechanical drum was built in 2009, and is on display in the museum of Villa Silvia in Cesena, Italy.

MACHINES FOR WORK AND PLAY
THE SELF-DRIVING CART

In 1478, more than four hundred years before the invention of the modern car, Leonardo sketched plans for the world's first self-driving vehicle. The cart was 1.58 m (5 ft) long and 1.49 m (4.9 ft) wide, with three wheels. It was propelled by a clockwork mechanism. This machine was so complex that no one could understand how it worked until well into the twentieth century.

A COPY OF LEONARDO'S ORIGINAL DRAWING OF THE CART'S MECHANISM

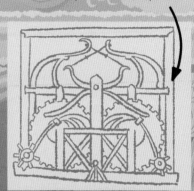

DRIVERLESS CART

Renaissance Robot
The cart had no seats and was not intended for the road. Historians believe da Vinci designed it for one of his wealthy patrons to show off to their guests. Being self-driving, some experts have called it the world's first robot!

1. The steering column featured a rack and pinion gear system, similar to that used in modern cars.

Springs, Wheels, and Pegs

The cart was powered by two springs. Rotating the wheels in a backward direction would wind up the springs. Then a brake was released and the cart would shoot forward. Experts believe it could travel up to 40 m (131 ft) before running out of power. The steering was programmed in advance. Pegs were placed in small holes to guide the wheels to turn at certain angles at moments during the journey. Oddly, it could only turn right!

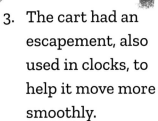

2. Two big leaf springs regulated the drive mechanism.

3. The cart had an escapement, also used in clocks, to help it move more smoothly.

It Works!

In 2004, a team of engineers at the Museum of the History of Science in Florence, Italy, decided to build the cart. They spent four months designing a digital model and then created a physical version at one-third of its size. They used five kinds of wood that would have been available to craftspeople in Leonardo's time. It took them eight months to build, and when they tested the machine, it worked perfectly! Next, they built a full-scale model, completed in 2006. To prevent damage to the full-scale version, they decided not to test it. Several observers noted its similarity to the Mars rovers *Spirit* and *Opportunity*.

THE ROBOTIC KNIGHT

Leonardo's lifelong interest in human anatomy may have inspired him to design one of the earliest known humanoid robots. Unlike most of his inventions, there is evidence that this one was actually built. The robot, dressed in a German-Italian medieval metal suit, was constructed in around 1495, and displayed at a party hosted by Duke Sforza of Milan. The guests must have been astonished when the machine began to move by itself.

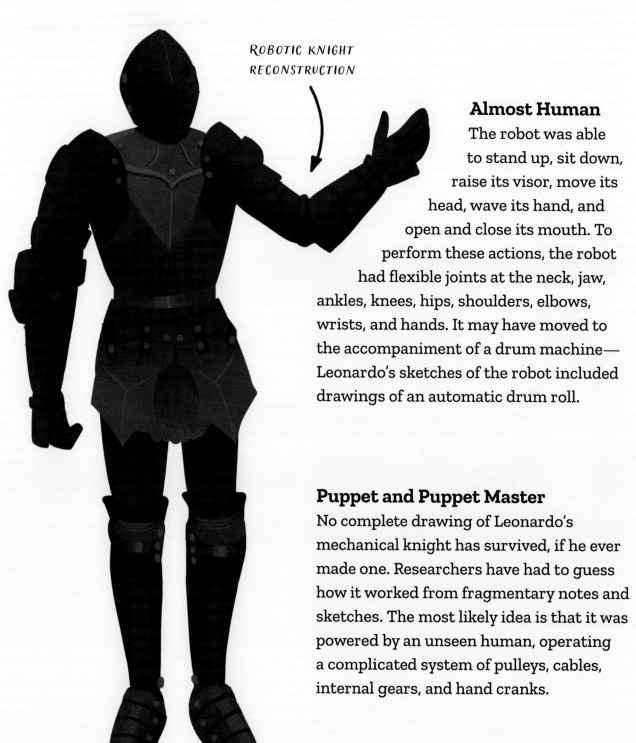

ROBOTIC KNIGHT
RECONSTRUCTION

Almost Human

The robot was able to stand up, sit down, raise its visor, move its head, wave its hand, and open and close its mouth. To perform these actions, the robot had flexible joints at the neck, jaw, ankles, knees, hips, shoulders, elbows, wrists, and hands. It may have moved to the accompaniment of a drum machine—Leonardo's sketches of the robot included drawings of an automatic drum roll.

Puppet and Puppet Master

No complete drawing of Leonardo's mechanical knight has survived, if he ever made one. Researchers have had to guess how it worked from fragmentary notes and sketches. The most likely idea is that it was powered by an unseen human, operating a complicated system of pulleys, cables, internal gears, and hand cranks.

Rosheim's Model

In 2002, American robotics expert Mark Rosheim used Leonardo's notes and drawings to build a working model of the knight. It worked beautifully, walking and waving with a smooth, fluid motion. In Rosheim's version, a computer in ithe knight's chest (rather than a hidden human) controlled the limbs, while electric motors (instead of cables) moved the muscles. Rosheim was so impressed by Leonardo's design of the robot's wrist that he went on to incorporate it in his design for NASA's Anthrobo—a robotic hand used to carry out tasks on Mars.

ROBOTIC LION

Robotic Lion

Leonardo designed several other robots, including a mechanical lion, which he presented to King Francis I in 1515. The lion, it is said, could walk ten steps, shake its head from side to side, open and close its jaws, and move its tail. A flap in the body opened to display a bunch of lilies, a symbol of French royalty.

MUSICAL INSTRUMENTS

Leonardo was an enthusiastic amateur musician who taught himself the lyre and could write his own songs. For him, music was the sister-art to painting, and had the same ability to, as he described it, "shape the invisible." He designed several unique musical instruments, including alternative versions of the flute, drum, hurdy-gurdy, and keyboard. He even invented a lyre in the shape of a horse's head!

Viola Organista

One of Leonardo's invented instruments was the viola organista. This fascinating creation combined elements of the harpsichord, organ, and viola da gamba—a type of stringed instrument. The player of the viola organista presses keys on a keyboard, which drives a friction belt that vibrates individual strings. The keyboard has forty-four keys with one string per key, or forty-four strings. It has a range of about three and a half octaves, typical of harpsichords of the time. As far as we know, the viola organista was never built, although similar instruments have been constructed over the years since.

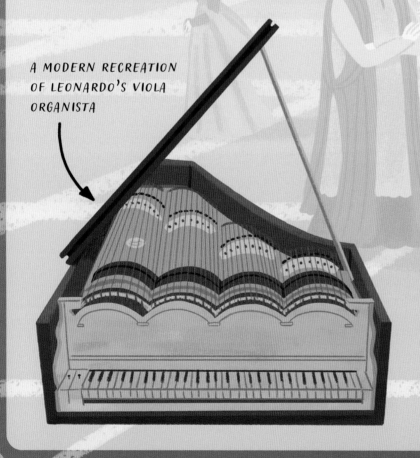

A MODERN RECREATION OF LEONARDO'S VIOLA ORGANISTA

Harpsichord-viola

Sketched by Leonardo in about 1488, this stringed instrument is played with a keyboard. It is smaller than the viola organista and designed to be mobile. The harpsichord-viola weighs about 15 kg (33 lbs) and is strapped to the musician's chest. It is powered by their legs as they walk, leaving their hands free to press the keys. The musician's legs pump a wooden motor, which causes a long strand of horsehair (like the bow of a violin) to loop continuously through the instrument. When the player presses the keys, the strings move against the horsehair, creating violin-like sounds. The harder the keys are pressed, the louder the sound. One of the unique features of this instrument is that it can play chords—something no other keyboard-operated instrument could do in Leonardo's day.

HARPSICHORD—VIOLA BEING PLAYED

Replica

In 2009, Japanese harpsichord maker Akio Obuchi constructed a replica of Leonardo's harpsichord-viola.

THE CLOCK

The first mechanical clocks were constructed in the 1270s. By Leonardo's day, clocks were becoming more accurate, though still primitive. For example, few of them had minute hands, let alone second hands. Leonardo designed a clock that was more accurate than any previously created. The mechanical principles of his clock are still used in the clocks we use today.

LEONARDO'S CLOCK

Designed for Time

Leonardo's clock had separate mechanisms for hours and minutes, each with their own intricate system of wheels, springs, gears, and levers. His clock also featured a separate dial for keeping track of the Moon's phases.

Fixing a Problem

Clockmakers in Leonardo's time had started to explore the use of springs rather than weights to power clocks. They developed a special pulley called a fusee to keep the spring's release even as it wound down; this was usually controlled by a piece of twine (strong string). The trouble was, the twine tended to stretch or break, making the clocks unreliable. Leonardo developed a device called a clock spring equalizer—an early form of escapement—to address this problem.

Pendulum

Leonardo was fascinated by pendulums and made many drawings of their motions, yet he never saw their potential for timekeeping. Pendulums didn't become part of clockmaking until 1656.

"Time stays long enough for those who make use of it."
Leonardo da Vinci

Finding Time

Perhaps Leonardo was attracted to clockmaking because he wished he had more time to work on his many projects! One way he carved out extra time for himself was to ration his sleep. He took thirty-minute naps every four hours, enabling him to work through the night. He even used a candle clock to keep track of time during the hours of darkness.

LEONARDO'S CANDLE CLOCK

Leonardo also invented an alarm clock in case he overslept during one of his naps. This was made up of two containers. Water flowed in a thin stream from one container to the other. When the second container was full, a system of gears, levers, and pulleys would raise Leonardo's feet into the air, waking him up!

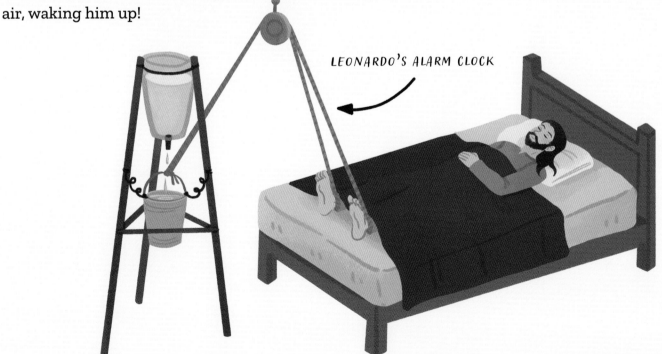

LEONARDO'S ALARM CLOCK

INDUSTRY MACHINES

Leonardo invented hundreds of devices over the course of his life, many of which were designed for practical uses, unlike his more famous, eye-catching machines. These included cranes, spinning machines, excavators, water-lifting devices, and hoists. He invented a file-cutting machine (a file is a tool for shaping and smoothing hard materials), an odometer (for measuring the distance journeyed by a wheeled vehicle), a printing press, and a compass.

Rolling Mill

In metalworking, rolling is a process in which metal is passed through a pair of rollers to reduce its thickness, make it uniform, or to give it a desired shape. In 1480, Leonardo sketched a machine made up of two parallel cylinders that would roll lead for stained glass windows. This was the first known design of a rolling mill in Europe. There is no evidence the device was ever built, but it established the basic design that all future rolling mills would follow.

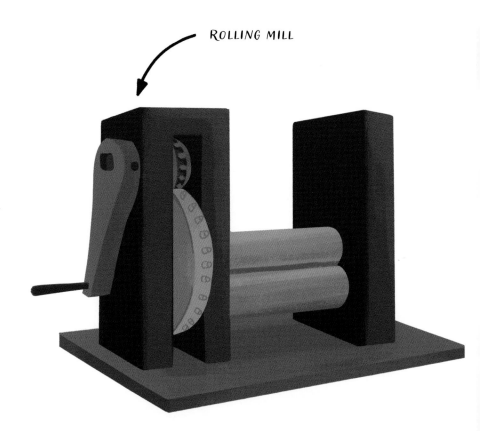

ROLLING MILL

Mirror Grinder

In Leonardo's day, there was a great demand for burning mirrors. These mirrors, when reflecting the Sun's rays, created a powerful, highly focused source of heat that could be used for tasks such as welding. The mirrors had to be concave with an even curvature, which was difficult and time-consuming when ground by hand, so Leonardo invented a device to automate the task. His mirror grinder used a rotating stone grinding wheel driven by a series of gears, which allowed for precise control over the grinding process.

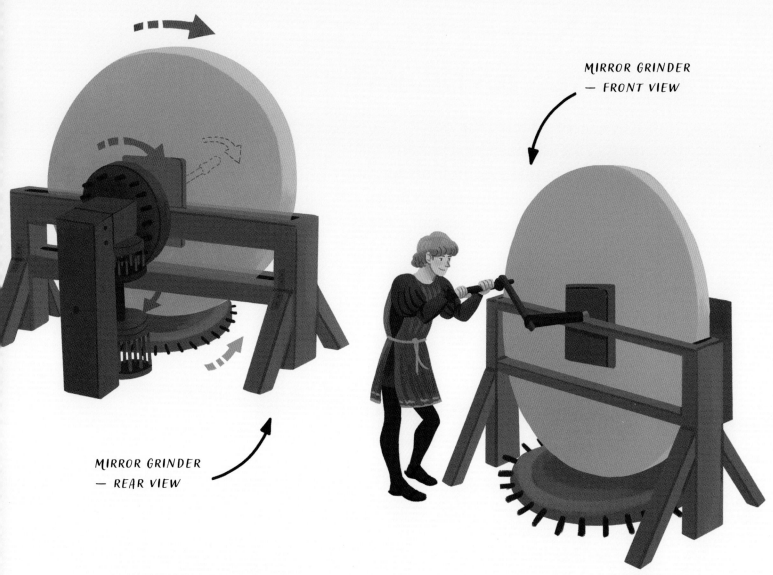

MIRROR GRINDER — FRONT VIEW

MIRROR GRINDER — REAR VIEW

Automatic Bobbin Winder

This machine was designed to wind thread or yarn onto bobbins for the weaving industry. Leonardo's sketch shows an exploded view to illustrate the component parts. The crankshaft rotates the bobbin, and the connecting rod moves the bobbin back and forth continuously so that the thread is wound evenly around it. It is one of the earliest recorded designs of a machine that could automate a repetitive task.

BOBBIN

AUTOMATIC BOBBIN WINDER

ART AND SCIENCE
PAINTINGS AND DRAWINGS

For hundreds of years after his death, Leonardo's fame rested not on his achievements as a scientist or as an inventor, but for his art. Fewer than twenty-five major paintings, including many unfinished works, and a few hundred drawings are attributed to Leonardo. However, they are some of the most influential works in Western art.

Famous Works

The *Mona Lisa*, Leonardo's greatest work, is probably the world's most famous painting. *The Last Supper* is the most reproduced religious painting of all time. *Salvator Mundi*, a painting attributed to Leonardo, is the most expensive painting ever sold at public auction. Leonardo's *Vitruvian Man* has become a symbol of humanism—a cultural movement of the Renaissance.

THE LAST SUPPER — RECREATION
OF LEONARDO'S PAINTING

Where Art and Science Meet

Leonardo's knowledge of science is evident in his paintings, just as it is in his inventions. His understanding of human anatomy—the structure of the muscles and bones beneath the skin—shows clearly in his portraits of people. His mastery of light gave his paintings a realism that was unusual for its time. It helped him invent a technique known as sfumato, in which blurred outlines and muted hues allow one form to merge with another, most notably in the *Mona Lisa*. Likewise, his studies of trees, plants, and water give his depictions of nature a remarkable authenticity. From his research into optics (the science of sight), he understood that we perceive the same hues differently depending on their distance, which is why the background mountains appear blue in his painting *Virgin on the Rocks*.

MONA LISA — RECREATION OF LEONARDO'S PAINTING

Vitruvian Man

Vitruvius, a famous Roman architect, suggested that the human body, with arms and limbs extended, should fit naturally inside a circle and a square. Many artists tried to prove this, but they used a circle and a square as their starting point, causing them to draw human figures with elongated limbs and small heads. Leonardo, with his scientific mind, decided to begin with the reality and work back toward the ideal. With his *Vitruvian Man*, he began with an accurate drawing of the human form, and then drew a circle and square to show how the body fit within it.

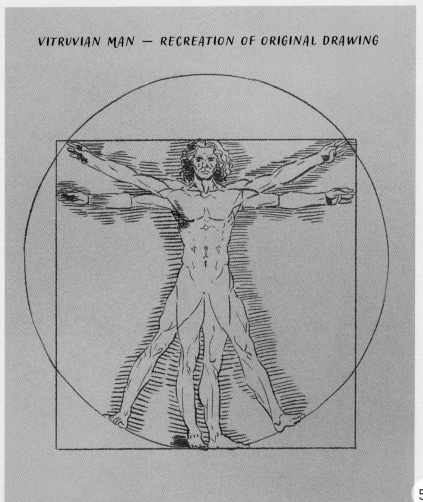

VITRUVIAN MAN — RECREATION OF ORIGINAL DRAWING

THE SCIENTIFIC METHOD

Leonardo's approach to science was to make careful observations and draw conclusions based on what he saw. This approach was similar to what later became known as the scientific method, followed by people such as Galileo and Newton.

"Before proceeding with an investigation, I will do some experiment, because my intention is to invoke the experience first and then demonstrate, with reasoning, why such experience must operate in such a way."
Leonardo da Vinci

Anatomy

Leonardo had studied human anatomy since his days working in Verrocchio's studio. Drawing the human body, he was able to picture the muscles, tendons, and bones—the visible structure of the body beneath the skin. During his life, he dissected 30 corpses and wrote an illustrated book on his theories. He was the first person to draw the appendix, lungs, and other organs in detail. He also made a number of important discoveries, including the way heart valves control the flow of blood.

A COPY OF LEONARDO'S DRAWING OF A HUMAN HEART

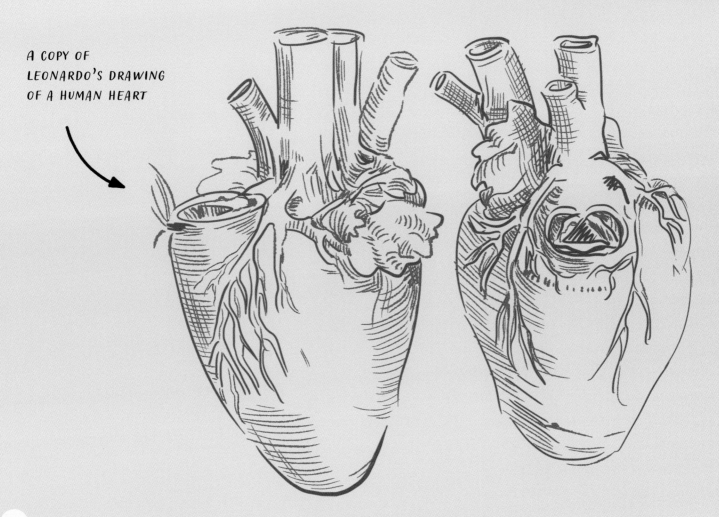

Optics

Leonardo's artistic training taught him about light, shadow, surfaces, reflection, and more. He created rules to explain how these different effects occurred. He rejected the false belief, common at the time, that humans could see due to rays beaming from our eyes, striking objects and bouncing images back to us. He came up with ideas for a projector, bifocals, and even contact lenses! He wrote about the telescope a century before it was invented. Leonardo compared eyesight to a camera obscura—a dark box or room with a tiny hole in one wall. The view of the outside world is projected upside down on the inside wall, directly opposite the hole. This comparison is surprisingly accurate.

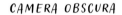
CAMERA OBSCURA

LEONARDO LOOKING
UP AT THE MOON

Astronomy

Leonardo believed, correctly, that the Moon reflects the Sun's light, and that anyone standing on the Moon would see earthlight just as we see moonlight from Earth. This contradicted the common view of the time that suggested moonlight came from the Moon itself. Leonardo also stated that "the Sun does not move," suggesting a belief in heliocentrism—that the Earth moves around the Sun and not the other way round, as was commonly believed in his day. It would be several decades before Copernicus became famous for making this same claim.

LEONARDO'S LEGACY
AIR AND WATER

Leonardo was fascinated by the motion of air and water. He was always looking at ways that we might make use of these elements and work with them. In his studies and experiments, Leonardo laid the groundwork for future scientific fields such as fluid dynamics (the study of how liquids and gases flow), hydraulics (the use of liquids for mechanical control), hydrology (the study of Earth's water and its movement), and the study of air flow and its effect on solid bodies.

LEONARDO STUDYING THE WING OF A DEAD BIRD

Birds and Flight

Leonardo examined how birds moved through the air to achieve flight. Through careful observation of wing motion, wind, air pressure, and gravity, he was able to work out how a bird remains stable in the air, alters its pitch, steers, and glides. He concluded, "A bird is an instrument operating through mathematical laws."

Leonardo believed these laws also applied to building a flying machine for humans, and while he was not able to create a working flying machine, many of his ideas influenced modern aircraft design. For example, the relationship between a curved wing section and lift; and the idea of air as a fluid.

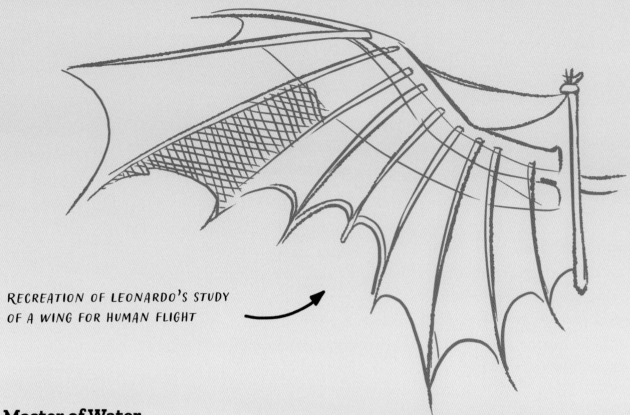

RECREATION OF LEONARDO'S STUDY
OF A WING FOR HUMAN FLIGHT

Master of Water

Leonardo was once described in the records of the Florentine government as a "Master of Water."
He himself would never lay claim to such a title, for he was aware of water's incredible power. But
he did seek to understand it and work with it. He investigated the ebb and flow of tides and the
destructive effects of water in erosion, floods, and storms. He explored ways to build canals and
divert rivers. He came close to the modern theory of the water cycle (the cycle of water from liquid
evaporated to form clouds, and then back to water as rain), and he learned that the same water
passes through rivers countless times. Although his writings on water were never published,
Leonardo was a pioneer in the study of this subject.

RECREATION OF LEONARDO'S
SKETCH SHOWING HOW
WATER FLOWS

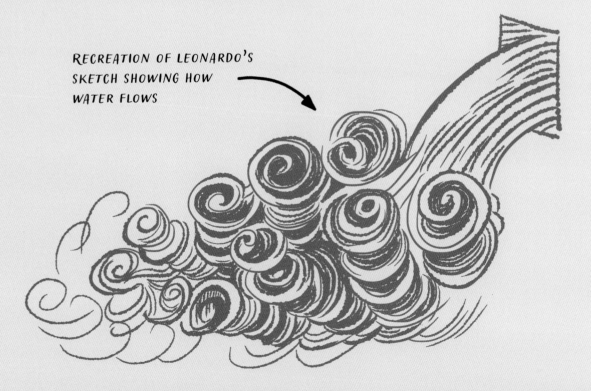

DRAWING TO INFORM

Leonardo invented technical drawing. That is, drawing to communicate complex ideas and information such as how a machine functions. Many of his sketches have influenced design plans and blueprints used by engineers today. How could someone who lived more than five hundred years ago invent a resource so useful to modern life?

Multiple Talents

Not only did Leonardo have a superb imagination, he also thought in systematic and logical ways. He had an almost otherworldly ability to see and solve technical problems, and he could envision (mentally picture) solutions. He was a gifted technical illustrator, and he knew how to use geometry and perspective to make his designs understandable to people.

New Ways to "See"

Leonardo invented many of the methods used in technical drawing today. These included plans with overhead views and drawings with cut-away views to reveal hidden mechanisms. He found ways of representing movement, force lines (the forces acting on a body), and variables (how adding or subtracting something will influence the performance of a machine).

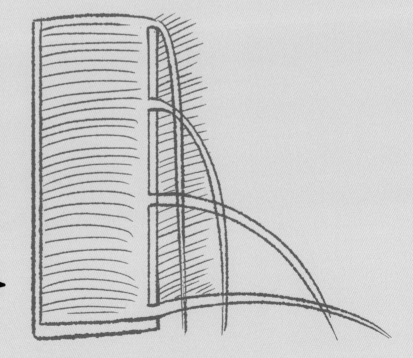

RECREATION OF LEONARDO'S DRAWING OF A WATER CONTAINER PIERCED BY HOLES
Leonardo drew this container of water pierced by holes at different heights to show how water pressure increases with depth. He was the first to use technical drawings to demonstrate different results based on changing variables.

Exploded Diagrams

One of Leonardo's innovations was the exploded diagram: a way of showing the individual components that make up a machine by disassembling them and pulling them apart. Through this method of drawing, he was able to show both the internal workings of a machine and the machine as a whole in a single drawing. Exploded diagrams are still widely used today.

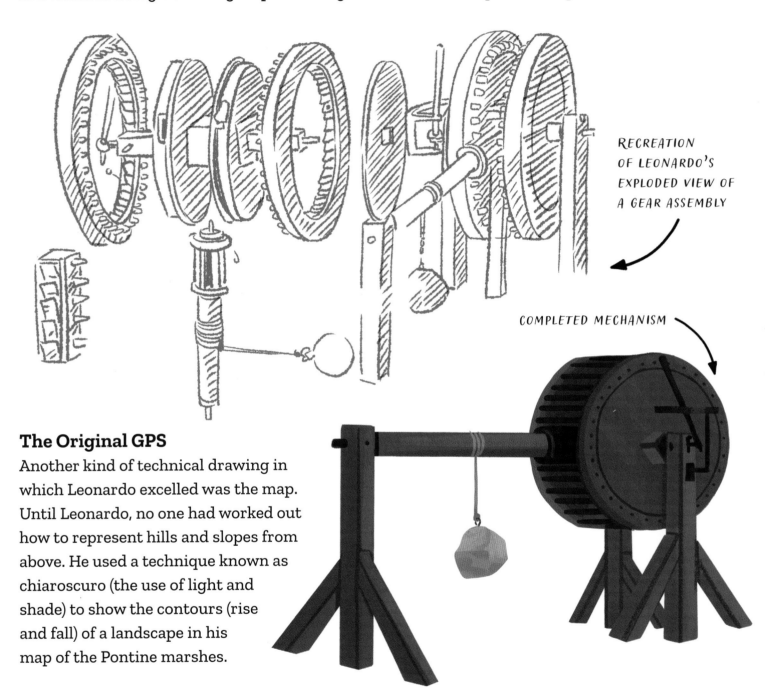

RECREATION OF LEONARDO'S EXPLODED VIEW OF A GEAR ASSEMBLY

COMPLETED MECHANISM

The Original GPS

Another kind of technical drawing in which Leonardo excelled was the map. Until Leonardo, no one had worked out how to represent hills and slopes from above. He used a technique known as chiaroscuro (the use of light and shade) to show the contours (rise and fall) of a landscape in his map of the Pontine marshes.

A Visual Language

Leonardo's technical drawings showed machines not as motionless objects but as dynamic, working devices. His drawings highlighted the importance of picturing a concept and creating a visual language through which inventors could communicate their ideas. This, as much as his inventions, was Leonardo's legacy.

CITY OF THE FUTURE

During the fifteenth century, Europe's cities were ravaged by frequent outbreaks of plague. With their narrow, dirty, and crowded streets, they were breeding grounds for infectious diseases. Transportation was also becoming a problem due to increasing congestion. Around 1486, Leonardo planned an ideal city of clean, open spaces, with a smooth-flowing transport system. Although it was never built, his ideas influenced urban planners of the future.

City in Layers

Leonardo imagined a city of some 30,000 inhabitants, built on the Ticino River in northern Italy. He proposed building the city on two levels. The upper level—with wide, well-ventilated streets, public squares, and elegant buildings— would be exclusively for pedestrians. "Only let that which is good-looking be seen on the surface of the city," he wrote.

The lower level would be used for trade, the transport of goods, and industry. Separating pedestrians from vehicles would reduce crowding and ease transportation. Buildings would rise through the lower and upper levels, giving access to both. The two levels would also be linked by external staircases.

Canal Streets

Being Leonardo, water played a vital role in his city plan. He proposed a network of canals, fed by the nearby river, running through the city's lower level. These would be used for transportation. Leonardo designed a system of locks and basins to allow ships to navigate them. The canals also functioned as a waste disposal system, with some of the water piped through buildings for internal plumbing. To avoid the risk of disease from stagnant water, he devised a system of hydraulic pumps to keep the canals flowing.

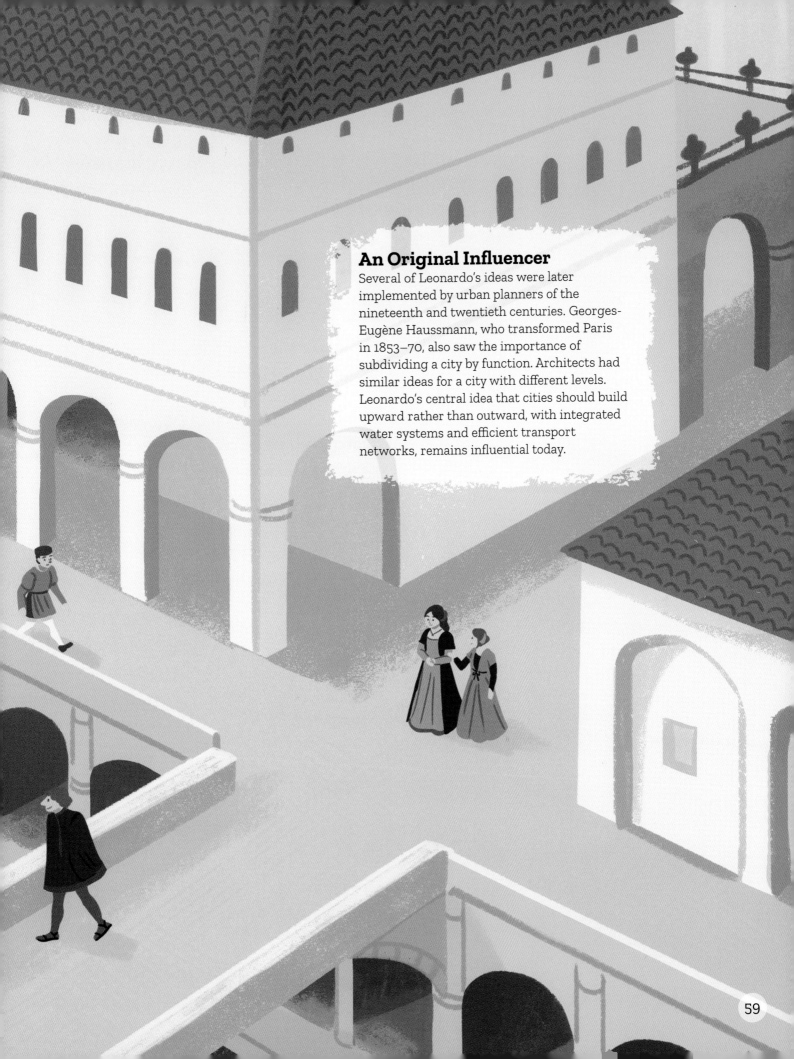

An Original Influencer

Several of Leonardo's ideas were later implemented by urban planners of the nineteenth and twentieth centuries. Georges-Eugène Haussmann, who transformed Paris in 1853–70, also saw the importance of subdividing a city by function. Architects had similar ideas for a city with different levels. Leonardo's central idea that cities should build upward rather than outward, with integrated water systems and efficient transport networks, remains influential today.

A PROGRESSIVE GENIUS

Leonardo's impact might have been far greater had his ideas been published and properly studied at the time, and been taken up by contemporary engineers. We might have had aircraft, diving suits, cars, and robots far sooner. As it is, his notes and drawings were destined to remain largely ignored by the scientific community for many centuries. By the time they were discovered, new materials, manufacturing methods, and sources of energy had been developed. As a result, his inventions were destined to be fascinating curiosities from a bygone age, rather than a key part of the history of technology.

Nature's Influence

Scientists continued to follow Leonardo's methods—particularly the way he viewed the natural world as inspiration for his inventions. Leonardo saw the parallels between animal anatomy and machines. He compared joints and tendons with hinges and winches, and muscles and bones with gears and levers.

ONE OF LEONARDO'S FLYING MACHINES NEXT TO A BAT IN FLIGHT

Leonardo's observations of birds in flight influenced his flying machines. The outer shell of his early tank is based on a turtle's shell. Falling seed pods from maple or sycamore trees perhaps led to his invention of the aerial screw, the predecessor of the helicopter. Today, we call this biomimicry—designing machines, materials, and systems with the help of nature's time-tested methods.

"Human subtlety will never devise an invention more beautiful, more simple, or more direct than does nature because in her inventions nothing is lacking, and nothing is superfluous."
Leonardo da Vinci

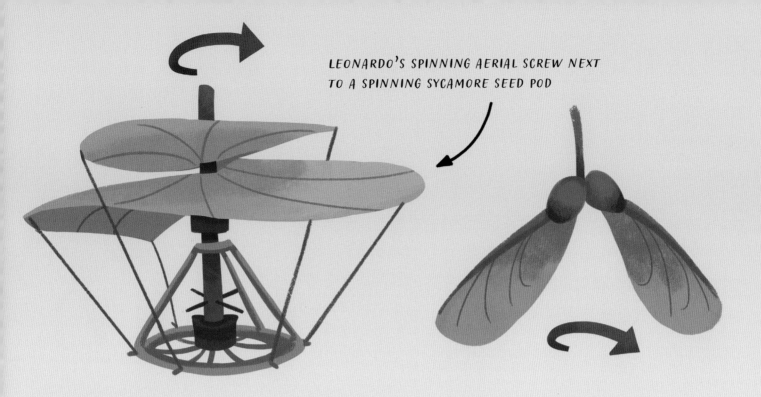

LEONARDO'S SPINNING AERIAL SCREW NEXT TO A SPINNING SYCAMORE SEED POD

Leonardo's Legacy

Leonardo set an example as someone with infinite curiosity, who was interested in everything around him, and had the energy to explore it all. As a scientist, he brought new techniques to painting; as an artist, he brought fresh creativity to scientific study; and as an engineer, he had the ability to research a problem and work to solve it in original ways that lit the path for future generations. Even though he lived more than five hundred years ago, Leonardo da Vinci continues to ignite our imaginations. He inspires us to ask questions, experiment, and find solutions to the challenges we face—no matter how difficult they may seem.

LEONARDO STUDYING THE WAVES IN THE SEA

GLOSSARY

ANATOMY The study of the structure of human and animal bodies.

APPRENTICE A person who learns a trade from a skilled employer.

ARCHITECT A person who designs buildings.

AXLE A rod that passes through the middle of a set of wheels.

BOBBIN A cylinder or cone that holds thread, used in weaving.

BOTANY The study of plants.

CHÂTEAU A large French country house or castle.

COUNTERBALANCE A weight that balances another weight.

CRANK An axle or shaft bent at right angles, for converting reciprocal (back-and-forth) motion to circular motion, or the other way round.

DISSECT Cut up a body to study its internal parts.

DIVING BELL An air-filled, open-bottomed chamber that supplies air to a diver.

DREDGER A boat designed to clear a river, or other area of water, by scooping out mud, weeds, and other garbage.

ENGINEER A person who designs, builds, or maintains machines or structures.

ESCAPEMENT A device in a clock, powered by a weight or spring, that checks and releases the gears by a fixed amount so that it moves at a regular speed.

FRICTION The resistance caused by one surface moving against another.

GAUGE A device that measures and shows the amount, level, or speed of something.

GEAR A toothed wheel that works with other toothed wheels to alter the speed or direction of other parts of a machine.

GEOLOGY The study of the Earth's physical structure.

GUILD An association of craftspeople common in medieval and Renaissance times.

HARPSICHORD A keyboard instrument with strings that are plucked when the keys are depressed.

HOIST An apparatus for raising or lifting something.

HYDRAULIC Describing a device that uses liquid under pressure as a source of power.

INCLINED PLANE A sloping ramp up which heavy loads can be raised by ropes or chains.

LEVER A rigid bar resting on a pivot, used to lift a heavy load attached to one end of the bar when pressure is applied to the other end.

LYRE A musical instrument that looks like a small, U-shaped harp.

MECHANICS The study of machinery.

MURAL A work of art painted directly on a wall.

OPTICS The study of sight and how light behaves.

PENDULUM A weight hung from a fixed point so it can swing freely, often used to regulate the mechanism of a clock.

PERIMETER The edge or boundary of an area, building, or object.

PERSPECTIVE The art of showing three-dimensional scenes or objects on a two-dimensional surface to give the right impression of their height, width, and depth.

PITCH The up-down, nose-to-tail motion of an aircraft or flying animal.

PIVOT The central point around which a mechanism turns.

PROPULSION The action of driving or pushing forwards.

PULLEY A wheel with a grooved rim around which a rope passes, which changes the direction of a force applied to the rope and which can be used to lift heavy weights.

RACK AND PINION A mechanism in which a toothed bar engages with a smaller cog (a wheel with a series of projections on its edge).

RENAISSANCE An era in European history from the 14th to the 17th centuries, which saw a revival of science, art, architecture, and music.

REPLICA A copy or model of something.

RUDDER A flat, hinged flap used for steering a boat or aircraft.

TECHNOLOGY The application of scientific knowledge for practical purposes, such as the development of machinery.

TRACTION The action of drawing or pulling something over a surface such as a road.

TREADMILL A large wheel turned by people or animals treading on steps fitted to the wheel's inner surface.

VACUUM A space from which the air has been removed.

VALVE A device for controlling the passage of liquid through a pipe.

WELDING Joining together metal parts by heating their surfaces until they start to melt.

WINCH A lifting device made up of a rope or chain winding around a rotating drum, usually turned by a crank.

INDEX

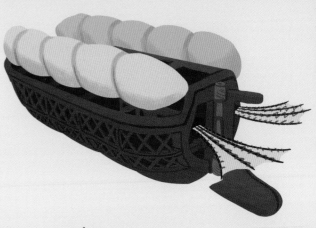

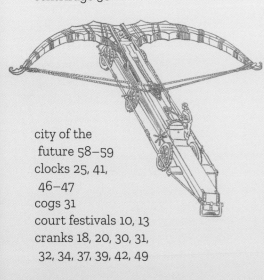